What people say al

What people say about Bad Boss

BAD

BOSS

7 Steps to Survive a Nightmare Boss

MICHAEL A. MILLER

Contents

Free Gift!

As a thank you for getting this book, I'd like to give you a free gift: a unique PDF called Leadership Strategies.

Go here now…

mikesbooks.space/bad-boss/

Enjoy!

Acknowledgments

I couldn't have written this book without the support of my wife, Joyce. I thank her for always being there and for also supporting me. I Love you, Joyce. It's been a great 37 years!

My thanks to Wayne Jenkins for his comments during one of our Effort Free Online Success training webinars. I added another Bad Boss to the mix because of Wayne's feedback.

Special thanks to my editor Doreen Martens. Her expert editing helped make this book a reality.

Thanks to Juan Garza, Valerie Iannuccilli, Bob Lewis, Jim Alty, and Ana Thiemer for reviewing an advance draft and offering their comments.

I also want to thank all the bosses I have had over the years, good and bad. I've learned a lot from all of you.

I would also like to acknowledge Chris Payne who is not only my book mentor, but just a great human being. His tutoring and constructive criticism were always carried out in a way that made me feel good about it. He has always taken the time needed to help me be successful. Thank you, Chris, for everything.

About the Author

Mike has had many Bosses during his 38-year career as a successful manager and leader. Some of the Bosses were good. Some OK. Some Bad.

Michael A. Miller

He has a bachelor's degree in engineering as well as an MBA. Mike is a lifelong learner and reader who looks for every opportunity to learn just a little more.

He is a John Maxwell certified trainer, speaker and coach in leadership and growth. Mike brings his experience and training to help others live a significant life.

Mike lives near Austin, Texas with his wife and two Scottish terriers.

1

Introduction

"What doesn't kill you makes you stronger."
— ***Friedrich Nietzsche***

They come in all shapes. They can be male or female. They are young and old. They can be short or tall. White, black or brown. They may be called CEO, president, director, manager, supervisor, foreman, etc. They have one thing in common. They are Bad Bosses.

A 2014 Gallup survey of 5,157 individuals discovered that just 10 percent of working people possess the ability to be a great manager and that the majority of supervisors in the U.S. are wrong for their job. (Winfrey G., 2015)

One reason is that many organizations base hiring decisions on the wrong criteria. Instead of selecting prospects who have the natural skills, or have received the necessary training needed for reliable leadership, organizations promote employees who have been with the organization for a long period of time and offer managerial jobs as a reward for solid performance in nonmanagerial duties. Most people just don't have the skills and abilities to be good bosses.

Here are some other eye-opening statistics from Brandon Gaille (Gaille, 2017):

- 75% of all employees say their boss is the worst part of their job
- Half of all employees who say they don't feel valued by their boss plan to look for another job
- American companies spend an estimated $360 billion annually on health care due to Bad Bosses
- Employees who have Bad Bosses are less productive
- 60% of Federal employees are unhappy because of their Bad Boss
- 65% of employees said they would rather have a new boss than a pay raise
- 37% of employees have bosses who fail to give them credit for work they do
- 44% of employees have been emotionally or physically abused by a Bad Boss during their career

There is a saying that people don't quit companies; they quit managers. The statistics bear this out. Bad Bosses can be infuriating and difficult to work for.

Working for a Bad Boss can be exhausting. You're unhappy, tired, irritable and unmotivated. Getting up each morning is a chore. You drag yourself to work. You dread that scheduled meeting with your boss and you jump if they walk by your desk or worksite. A Bad Boss leaves you frustrated, angry and often confused. You may even get physically ill. Tension headaches, ulcers, high blood pressure, insomnia, indecision and even depression can all be the result of a Bad Boss.

Most of us will put up with a Bad Boss because we need to make a living. We have a mortgage or rent to pay, as well as car payments, need to eat, want to go on vacation, have others to support, and have bills to pay. So we trudge on and put up with things we probably shouldn't. We hope that things will get better, but they never do. It's difficult to complain to Human Resources since they often take the boss's side. Quitting your job is even harder since you have responsibilities, and job hunting is tough even in the best of times.

This book is about those Bad Bosses. The Bad Boss categorizations and suggestions for what to do when confronted with one are based upon careful research and over 35 years of experience. But keep in mind that not all bosses react the same way. Some may not be open to the Seven Steps in dealing with your nightmare boss provided here. So consider carefully as you implement them.

As you read through this book, remember that you cannot change Bad Bosses. They need to change themselves. However you can use the techniques in this book to help them realize the need for change or to help you find a way to adjust and find some peace at work.

Throughout this book I use *they* instead of *he* or *she*. My main reason is because Bad Bosses can be male or female.

This book will help you identify what kind of Bad Boss you have. It will provide tips on how to live with your Bad Boss and find your way to a happier life. But don't skip the work. Everything good comes at a cost and. in this case, you need to work hard to develop that good relationship with your boss.

2

Who Are the Bad Bosses?

"And if the blind lead the blind, both shall fall into a pit."
— Matthew 15:14, The Bible, English Standard Version

There are many types of Bad Bosses. You can probably think of a dozen or more, but I have summarized them into seven distinctive groups. Here they are:

- Deer in the Headlights
- Control Freak
- The Bully
- Optics Freak
- My Buddy
- Outlaw
- The Ogre

Don't be surprised to find that your boss fits into more than one category. Most bosses have traits that overlap. But they normally have a predominant tendency.

Deer in the Headlights

Maybe you have driven down a dark road and seen a deer standing in the middle. It just stands there, eyes reflecting your car lights back at you, rather than getting out of the way. The Deer in the Headlights Bad Boss is like this. They simply do not know what to do. They don't take action.

 The Deer is one of the most common types of Bad Boss. As mentioned in the Gallup survey, only 10% of all managers are really equipped to be good managers. The remaining 90% suffer from a lack of training and, in some cases, simply a lack of ability.

Often, this type of boss has done a good job in a technical or support position and was promoted up because of that good performance. But no training was provided, they do not know how to supervise. As a result, they are completely out of their depth.

Deer bosses do not communicate well. They can answer a technical question but often are at a loss when it comes to anything else. I had a boss one time who, when I asked what I should do about a particular personnel issue, simply said, "I don't know." While I admire that truthfulness, we look to our bosses for advice and guidance.

Some Deer will try to "bluster" their way through by acting as though they know what they are doing when they clearly don't. Some are very good actors. Some will take on traits of the Buddy and try to make their employees their friends because they don't know what else to do.

The Control Freak

The Control Freak is also known as the micromanager. They want to control every aspect of their job and yours. They proofread your work, want to be copied on all your emails and are constantly offering "helpful" suggestions, relaying orders, or asking for continual updates.

I actually had a boss who wanted to be copied on all emails. They said they just wanted to help me, but the concern was really about having things done their way. It drove me crazy. The Control Freak's motto is often "My way or the highway."

Control Freaks tend to focus on the smallest possible details, which sometimes means overlooking the big picture. They are more concerned with dotting i's and crossing t's than accomplishing what needs to be done.

It can be a good thing to have a Control Freak in charge, for those new employees who need a lot of structure in their daily work. But for people who like to work independently and are self-motivated, the Control Freak can be frustrating to work for.

If you like to take a project, work on it and run with it without being constantly asked questions and given directions, the Control Freak is not for you. You will get frustrated and stressed very quickly.

The Bully

We all know what a bully is. They are someone who pushes other people around. Bully types can be further subdivided into Old Yeller, Put-Down Artist and Passive-Aggressive types.

The Bully typically knows exactly what they are doing and the impact it has on the employee. The problem is they just don't care. The effects on an employee can be worse than that of any other type of Bad Boss. The abuse and intimidation, the put-downs, and demeaning comments can all be difficult to deal with and eat away at your self-esteem.

The Old Yeller type of Bully likes to yell and scream, often for no reason at all and at any moment. You've probably had one of these or know someone who has. Old Yeller doesn't scream just once or twice, but often, and typically without provocation. Somebody who raises their voice occasionally while having a rare bad day is not an Old Yeller.

An Old Yeller just wants to be heard. That is one reason they feel the need to speak over everyone else. They may think you are not listening. They may be stressed out. It could be that the only way they know to deal with the stress of their job is yelling. You are not necessarily the reason for their anger. They feel pressure from above or from home. They may be pushing themselves too hard or have a demanding boss of their own. They may not even know what they're doing.

However, none of these reasons change the fact that their yelling is aimed at you. Yelling is a form of bullying and aggressive behavior that has no place in the workplace.

The Put-Down Artist Bully can be a very difficult kind of boss to deal with since their behavior can get very personal. This type of bully uses negative reinforcement and insults to get what they want done. They constantly talk down to you and generally have nothing good to say. Don't plan on getting positive feedback from this type of individual.

The Passive-Aggressive Bully likes to try to control you indirectly, using stubborn or other negative behaviors such as procrastination. A passive-aggressive boss may say things like "Did I hear that right?" or "You did really well on that project, but…" or "It's not personal." You get the picture.

Passive-Aggressive bullies may try to prevent a change or dismiss a suggestion that will improve the workplace, especially if it comes from a subordinate. They may fear competition from you and will not let a subordinate be seen as better than they are. They may sulk and intentionally "forget" what you told them. The passive-aggressive bully may also blame others rather than take responsibility. The behavior of these bosses is often the result of a fear of rejection, mistrust, insecurity, or low self-esteem.

I have run into a number of Passive-Aggressive Bullies. One in particular, who was also a Deer, would often go around his supervisor and talk to the boss above. He would provide all sorts of information and misinformation that did nothing but destroy the relationship between him and his immediate supervisor.

Another boss I had would smile a lot but make little effort to communicate with me. This boss ended up going directly to my staff to accomplish what they wanted, without even letting me know.

The Optics Freak

Optics Freaks are narcissists, people who care only about themselves. They focus on how things look instead of how things are or could be. They often take on many of the characteristics of the Control Freak.

They don't pay attention to the impact their behavior or decisions have on others. They are interested only in hearing good things about themselves and their performance. They tend to be closed to any feedback from their peers or subordinates. They can do no wrong and often take credit for others' work. They will often play the martyr.

The focus of Optics Freaks is on how they look to others. It is "all about the optics" to them. Now, it is fine to be concerned about presenting a good image and doing your best, but it can go too far when every action is judged by how it will make the boss look to others. The Optics Freak is overly concerned about reputation, believing it is of paramount importance. Consequently, they will push others around, much like a Bully, to get what they want without regard to anyone else.

I recall one Optics Freak boss who wanted daily meetings and reports so that he knew everything that was going on. He would frequently remind everyone that it was all about the optics.

You can feel frustrated with the Optics Freak boss, especially, when you spend all of your time doing tasks that do not contribute to the overall project but make them look good. You will never be good enough for your Optics Freak boss. They will make you feel inferior and inept.

My Buddy

OK, admit it. We all have thought at some time that the boss has favorites. Anita gets all the best assignments. Bob is always allowed to go out of town to conferences. Juan gets to work a flexible schedule. It's just not fair.

My Buddy is the person who wants to be everyone's friend. The My Buddy boss may want to talk throughout the day, inquire about your personal life, and even get together outside of work.

Of course, you want to gain your boss's trust and respect and engaging in personal conversations with them can be a wise investment but be sure to establish boundaries. Be aware of co-workers who may become jealous and feel that you are receiving special treatment if you and your boss become too friendly.

25

That said, there are bosses out there that do have favorites. Instead of picking someone for a choice assignment or trip because of their skills, abilities and experience, they pick the person they like the most. This bias may also be reflected in performance evaluations, reviews, projects, etc.

It's tough and demotivating to work for someone who is constantly ignoring your contribution or not allowing you to have a crack at a choice assignment.

The Outlaw

There isn't a lot to say about the Outlaw boss. These are the bosses who think rules and laws do not apply to them. They may break organizational rules and norms. They may even believe that they can get away with breaking the law or government regulations.

I have seen this on several occasions, especially where it comes to pay. They do what they want, when they want and how they want.

Be careful to not be drawn into their schemes. You don't want to end up in trouble. You could lose your job or go to jail.

Here are just some examples of how they can break rules and laws:
- Ignoring company hiring practices
- Deviating from established procedures

- Mistreating employees
- Ignoring safety rules and regulations
- Working their staff without overtime pay
- Illegal discrimination
- Sexual harassment

Of course, there are lots more.

These are bosses to stay clear of. You don't want to get drawn into their improper and sometimes illegal activities. Make sure you tread carefully around them.

The Ogre

The Ogre is the absolute worst Bad Boss you can have. No, they don't live under a bridge, but they may be any of the above types or a combination of two or more. What makes them the worst is that they are hopeless. These are Bad Bosses that will not respond positively to the Seven Steps. In this case, you may have to move to Chapter 10 – The Nuclear Option.

3

The Seven Steps

"Peace is not the absence of conflict, but the ability to cope with it."
— ***Mahatma Gandhi***

So, now it's time to apply the Seven Steps. This is where the work begins. Don't expect to go through these steps in a short period of time. You will need to work on each one, review it and revise it before moving to the next.

The Seven Steps include:
1. Evaluate
2. Review possible strategies
3. Develop and implement a plan
4. Get support
5. Implement your plan
6. Reassess
7. Adapt and Repeat

Only you can decide if your boss will respond positively to the Seven Steps. There are no guarantees. After going through the steps once, you may need to make significant changes so that they work for you.

The following chapters will detail what you should do in each of these steps.

4

Evaluate

"Don't find fault, find a remedy."
— Henry Ford

This is one of the most important steps. The Evaluate step involves defining the problem, gathering information and analyzing that information to see how it can help you understand what's going on at a deeper level. Once you understand the situation with all its variables and motivations, you can devise a plan.

As you go through this step, keep in mind that your Bad Boss is a human being. They have their own faults. They are not perfect. They will make mistakes. They will get angry. Despite all of this, make sure to treat your boss with the same basic respect every human being is entitled to.

Also, remember that you are a human being, too. You will make mistakes. You have your own faults. Self-reflection is a good technique when dealing with a Bad Boss. Take some time to think about your interactions with your boss and whether or not you may be contributing to the situation. Do you have some responsibility here? Then take it.

Start gathering some notes. Document what happens in your interactions with your boss, especially if things are bad.

Write down your thoughts, using a tablet, piece of paper or your own laptop. Don't document on company time, but on your break, lunch hour, or at home. Do not use a company computer or telephone to record your notes. You want to keep yourself above reproach during this process. Keep your documentation at home.

Do not record conversations. Many organizations have policies about recording conversations, and you can be disciplined or even terminated for doing so. In addition, many jurisdictions require notification or consent of both parties before recording a conversation.

Make sure to document any illegal activities. If there is supporting documentation and it is not against organizational rules for you to have it, then include it with your documentation. You may need it later if you need to go to Human Resources or file a legal complaint.

Above all, take the high road. Be truthful and ethical. Do not compromise yourself. It just isn't worth it. I have, on a couple of occasions, had to tell my boss that I would not do something because I believed it compromised my Professional Engineering license. They accepted that and backed down.

Once you have your notes and documentation together, sit down and answer these questions:

- What is it my boss is doing that I don't like?
- Am I doing something to contribute to the situation?
- What type of Bad Boss do I have?
- What are the sources of conflict between us?
- What is it that triggers my boss's behavior?
- How do I feel when my boss acts negatively?
- Are there illegal activities going on?
- Are organizational rules or laws being violated?
- What actions can I take to help improve the situation?
- What solutions can I offer?
- Are others experiencing the same thing, or is it just me?

Think of other questions that you may need to answer and add them to the list. Once you have your notes, documentation and answers together, you will need to consider the strategies you can use in dealing with your Bad Boss.

5

Review Possible Strategies

"People don't leave bad jobs; they leave Bad Bosses."
— Unknown

Several strategies can be used to deal with a Bad Boss. You will use these strategies in Step 3, where you will develop a plan. As you review these potential strategies, remember that no one strategy will work on every type of Bad Boss. There are no guarantees. It may be necessary to use a combination of strategies to be successful in changing the situation.

Don't be tempted to ignore the Seven Steps and simply try a strategy or two. While the strategies may help you feel better immediately, they will not provide long-lasting relief from your situation. You need the Seven Steps to make lasting progress.

The following sections provide some strategies you can consider using depending on your situation.

Acknowledge

Acknowledge that you understand what your boss is saying. A good tactic would be to rephrase what they are saying and repeat it back to them. In this way, your Bad Boss will see that you are paying attention and really listening.

Avoidance

Avoid your Bad Boss. Stay away. Hide. However, avoiding will not alleviate the problem. The issues remain. But avoidance may provide some temporary relief when you really need it. Use it sparingly.

Be Appreciative

If you have a Control Freak boss, you can show appreciation for their guidance, as misguided as it may be, while gently letting them know you have things under control yourself. You both want to see the best work produced.

Confide

Find a colleague or friend to confide in. It might help to get a different perspective from another person or simply be able to vent in a safe environment.

Communicate

The best way to deal with any boss is to communicate. Communicate. Communicate. Communicate. This one little thing causes 80% of problems at work and at home.

Communicating will help ease your boss's mind and provide them with a sense that you know what you are doing.

A big part of the Seven Steps is communicating with your Bad Boss if you can.

Do Your Best and be Professional

Do your best to give 100% to your job. Remember, your boss is not your friend. Their job is to provide you with tasks to accomplish and to monitor your progress. Behave in a professional manner. Do not raise your voice. Do not swear. Be polite. Do not lose your cool.

Follow Through

Make sure to follow through on what the boss asks you to do and to ask for advice along the way if needed. This will send the message that you are paying attention and doing your best to meet their expectations. It's possible that being diligent may calm down the Bad Boss a little, since they know you are listening. However, be careful not to ask for advice too often, or they may think you don't know what you are doing.

Instead, have a discussion about how often they would like to be updated, and ask questions there during the talk. Try sitting down with your Bad Boss and asking how you can be more in tune with their needs.

Help Make Your Bad Boss A Better Supervisor

One of the best courses of action for the Deer in the Headlights type is to try to help your Deer become a better supervisor. You may actually be able to take on an informal leadership role with the Deer so that they can learn from you.

Let Your Boss Know What You Can Do

Especially with the Control Freak, issues can be the result of your boss lacking knowledge of your abilities. Make sure they understand your skills and your competencies. It's possible they may not know your background. When discussing an assignment, you may be able to say, "Hey, I did that in my last job." Or you might sit down with your boss and explain that you want them to know how you can help, and then discuss your background.

Meeting

An excellent thing to do is meet with your Bad Boss to discuss your working relationship. You can use the plan you develop and the Seven Steps to guide this conversation. (More on meeting with your boss later.) Do not be confrontational. Stay calm. Have your bullet points written out ahead of time.

Reassess

This is also a step in the Seven Steps, but it doesn't hurt to spend a little time assessing what you like about your job. Maybe it's great pay or benefits. Maybe it's your co-workers. Taking a step back and thinking about what you are grateful for may help.

Set Boundaries

It's OK to have a friendly relationship with your boss, but don't let it go too far. Set boundaries. Be respectful. Decline social invitations in a polite way.

Updates

Be proactive and have a discussion about how and when your Bad Boss wants updates or briefings. Set up regular meetings to discuss your projects or work and what their expectations are. Update your Bad Boss at these meetings and try to get some feedback.

Always have an agenda for the meeting, to show you are organized and know what you're doing. Finally, keep notes. This can be invaluable.

I had an experience where my boss questioned whether or not I had received permission for a particular purchase. They claimed I had not talked about it with them. I knew I had. I found my agenda and notes, which proved we had spoken about it and I did receive permission.

Taking the initiative to do this assures your Bad Boss that the two of you will discuss your projects on a regular basis. That may make your boss less inclined to be constantly asking for updates and giving direction.

Other Things to Remember

Generally speaking, there is no rule that says your boss has to be nice. Well, that's not really true. No good organization will put up with a Bad Boss for long. There are simply too many risks. Not only will productivity suffer, but there is a risk of Federal laws being broken if discrimination takes place.

Most Importantly

Do not give up your moral beliefs or your personal code of ethics. Crossing this line goes too far and you will regret it. If you think your boss is asking you to do something that goes against your beliefs, talk with them. If you still believe this is true and they are insisting, go to Human Resources or their boss.

6

Develop A Plan

"For tomorrow belongs to the people who prepare for it today."
— ***African Proverb***

You have gathered all of your information. You sat down and considered a number of questions. It's time to put all of that information into a concise plan, so as to move forward with the ultimate aim of meeting and discussing your concerns.

Use the strategies outlined in the previous chapter to determine the action steps you will take. Remember that you may need more than one strategy.

Here is a general outline of what your planning might include:
- Write out your plan
- Determine your type of boss
- My goal is/my boss's goal is _____
- The negative behaviors my boss exhibits are _____
- Those negative behaviors make me feel _____
- Here is what I may be doing to contribute to the situation _____
- Here are some solutions I thought of _____
- Here are the strategies I will use _____
- How will I implement these strategies?

Remember to stay focused on solving the problem as you write up your plan. Do not get personal. This is not about your boss as a person, but about their interactions and behaviors with you. Add any factors that you think might be relevant.

Where possible have one or two examples for each of the points in your plan.

Write Out Your Plan

Just as you did in the evaluation step, you'll want to write your plan down. The difference now is that you want to take all of the information you gathered and condense it down into one or two pages. At this point, you will choose the strategies you will use and work them into your plan as you develop a series of action steps.

Take your time as you write things down and do so in concise and simple language. I suggest using of bullet points to keep things simple. Set it down and walk away for a day or two. When you come back to it, go back and revise it as needed. Be sure to take the emotion out, other than to list how you feel about the negative behavior. Do not include accusations or put-downs.

This is your plan, something you can use to guide the meeting you might decide to have with your boss. You are not going to show your plan to your boss, but you may want to discuss it if you decide to meet. In the next step, you will discuss your plan with a confidant, friend, spouse, or trusted co-worker.

Type

Write down the type(s) of boss you have. This will help you gather your thoughts. Reread the descriptions of the various types of bosses discussed in Chapter 2 and narrow yours down to a primary type.

Negative Behaviors and Feelings

What are the negative behaviors that your boss exhibits, and how do they make you feel? You might write down "She/he yells and me, and I feel afraid and worthless when that happens." Understand the feelings those negative behaviors create.

You have a right to feel the way you do, and your boss should not discount your feelings. If they do, they may be worse than you thought.

Goals

Here are some questions to think about:
- What is your goal?
- What do you hope to achieve at work?
- Why do you work?
- What is your ideal outcome for this situation?
- What would you accept as an outcome?

Consider these questions as you determine your goal and write it down. For example: Do you want to feel needed? Do you simply want the micromanaging to stop and be respected for what you know? You may want to list several such goals and then settle on one in particular. Keep it simple.

What goals do you think your boss wants to achieve? They may want to make sure that work is done on time and in a professional way. They may want all the attention (Optics Freak). They may actually want harmony in the workplace.

What would a common goal be? You both want something, and there will probably be some overlap. Maybe it's just to have a better understanding of each other or to move towards a more respectful work environment. Be prepared to discuss this with your boss.

Your boss will want something also. You need to be ready to give. Chances are they also want to work more smoothly with you. They do not need the hassle of a disgruntled employee. So, think carefully about what their goals may be and write them down.

My Contribution

None of us is perfect. As the saying goes, there are always two sides. Write down a list of things you may have done to contribute to the situation or what you could have done differently. Do you treat your boss the way they treat you?

Do you avoid saying "Good morning"? I was shocked once when I was told that I didn't say "good morning" and that was a negative. However, I corrected that behavior, and it improved my relationships with my staff.

Maybe you didn't give that last task your complete attention. There is nothing wrong with admitting that you carry some responsibility for the situation.

Solutions and Strategies

This is a very important part of planning. In Step 2, you looked at various potential strategies and solutions. It's now time to select those you want to move forward with.

What strategies and solutions do you think are reasonable to implement? Make a bullet list. Be sure that you have a list of your expectations of your boss as well as a list of what you are prepared to do in return. Start with what you want to do to help the situation. Think about how the two of you can work together better.

Lay out what strategies you plan to use and how you are going to use them.

Finally

Put your plan aside. In a safe place. You will want to give this process some time, and then go back and revisit it. Revise, adjust and edit. You may want to do this several times. Take your time to get it right. It is very important to the success of your meeting with the boss.

7

Get Support

"Alone we can do so little; together we can do so much."
— Helen Keller

Another set of eyes never hurts. You need to have someone review your plan and give you a different perspective. Make sure that whoever you talk with is trustworthy and will not let your conversation get back to others. Some possibilities include a spouse, friend, or a trustworthy co-worker.

Choose wisely when picking this person. You don't need to get the rumour mill involved. I've always said that the only thing faster than the speed of light is the rumor mill.

Sit down with confidant in a quiet place where you won't be disturbed and let them know what you are going through. Explain that you need them to keep this confidential. Let them know you are following a process to try to resolve the issues, and one of those was to develop a plan and ask for input from someone else.

Go through your plan with them. Explain each point. Let them ask questions. Listen carefully. Take notes. You will want to listen to their feedback and consider whether or not to include it in your plan. Remember that listening is part of communication.

If you are going to meet with your boss, role-play the meeting with your trusted friend, spouse, etc. This will help you prepare. Take turns being boss-employee and employee-boss. Playing the role of the boss may open your eyes to some dynamics. Make notes about how things went and suggestions you both came up with. Even if you are not going to actually meet with your boss, the role-playing may be an important exercise.

After you complete this step, be sure to go back and revise your plan as needed. This is critically important. You want to take what you learned and incorporate it into your plan. If you think it would be helpful, repeat this process with another trustworthy friend or colleague.

8

Implement Your Plan

*"The single biggest problem in COMMUNICATION is the
illusion that it has taken place."*
— George Bernard Shaw

At this step you will implement your plan. If you decide that
avoiding your Bad Boss is all you can do, then this will be
when you do it. If you plan on having daily meetings,
implement them. Many strategies are easy to implement and
others much harder. While developing your plan and
considering strategies, you should have thought about and
written down how you would implement each and every
strategy you expect to use.

However, the greatest opportunity for permanent change
comes with communication. So, the remainder of this chapter
will be devoted to meeting with your boss.

Meeting with Your Bad Boss

The big day is here. You have put together all of your
documentation, evaluated it and put together a plan to guide
your meeting. You have reviewed your plan with someone
else.

Now set up a meeting with your boss. An hour should be enough. If it threatens to go long, ask to schedule a second meeting. You can say you want to meet to make sure you are doing what you need to do, and to improve your working relationship. You need time to process the information you discuss.

Your plan will be your guide through the discussion. Be ready to deviate if need be but try to stick to the plan. Be assertive, but not aggressive. Be respectful and professional. No personal attacks. Don't argue with your boss; it will get you nowhere and it will appear that you are on the defensive.

Set boundaries with your boss, by gently letting them know what those boundaries are. Also, set boundaries for yourself. Know your limits and identify what you need to do when your Bad Boss crosses those. Be prepared to end the meeting early if things are not going well. You may just want to say, "I have a lot to think about and need some time," or "I need to use the restroom." You may need time to regroup.

You do not want to go point by point from your plan. The plan is there to help you gather your thoughts. Do not tell your boss that they are an "Old Yeller."

You can start by saying you have some concerns and you want to make sure you are meeting their needs. State your work goals and offer up that you need the boss's help to achieve them. Ask what their goals are and discuss ways that the two of you can meet the common goal. This involves listening, communicating, and brainstorming together.

Discuss any barriers to the common goal. This would be the place where behavior on both sides is discussed. Be ready to admit your flaws. This is also the time to gently mention behaviors your boss has and how they make you feel. You might say, "Mr. Garcia, when you yell at me, I feel upset and like I'm not part of the team," or "Ms. Scott, I had a lot of experience at this kind of job before and I want to do it your way, but when you come and check on me constantly, I get nervous and find it hard to get anything done. Can you help?"

Once there is an understanding of the possible problems, it's time to offer up solutions. Be the first to do so. Tell your boss what you think you can do to help the situation. Ask what they think.

Develop three or four action items that the two of you can work on. Maybe weekly meetings, or a different work assignment. Agree to both work on it and schedule a follow-up.

Be prepared to listen and ask questions where you need to. This is vitally important. Also, take notes. You want a record of the meeting and the results.

9

Reassess

"Experience is the teacher of all things."
— **Julius Caesar**

So, you've implemented your strategies. Some worked and some didn't. Now is the time to reassess.

Take your plan out and read it through again. Look at your strategies. For each one, what worked and what didn't? What could you have done better? Why did those that didn't work fail? Think about whether or not each strategy is working and whether you want to continue to use it or discard it.

Meeting with Your Bad Boss

So, let's say you decided to meet with your boss. The meeting is over. One of two things happened. It went well or it did not. Either way, you learned a lot. You now know where you stand, but now you need to use that information to reassess to your situation.

If it went well, then there is hope. If your boss was open to discussing how to improve the work environment and your relationship, then you may be on your way, to a better relationship and relief from the stress you were under.

Consider what you both discussed and what it means to you. What did you learn? How does it change your outlook?

OK, maybe it did not go well. This means one of two things: your plan needs revising, or your boss is an Ogre. This type of boss is the one you cannot reason with. There is no solution to that will improve your relationship.

If you think there may be some hope, reassess your situation. Think about your meeting and what happened during that time.

Ask yourself some questions:
- What went wrong in the meeting? Why?
- What could I have done differently?
- What behaviors do I need to change?
- What did my boss really say?
- What was the meaning of what he said?
- What positives can I take from the meeting?

Consider all of this and go on to the next step.

10

Adapt And Repeat

"The measure of intelligence is the ability to change."
— Albert Einstein

You have sat down and reassessed your relationship with your boss. This helped you identify what you can change in the interest of having a better relationship. Change is a continuous process and that is what you are trying to accomplish here. You want to change your interactions with your boss.

Adapt

Adapt to any changes you need to make to improve your relationship and then go back to Step 1 and begin again. Use the ideas you came up with by reassessing the situation to adapt once again.

Adapting can be difficult. It means you will have to change. It means you may need to develop new habits. We humans don't like change, even though change is the one constant in life. Everything changes.
The best way to change is to develop new habits. Try using an app for your iPhone or Android that helps develop new habits.

There are many. I use Habit Bull. You may want to set a goal of simply saying "Good morning" to your boss every day or updating them on your current project status. Regardless, developing new habits is crucial to cementing the changes you need to make.

Repeat

Add your most recent information to your documentation. Answer the questions anew. You might be surprised that some of the answers change. Then re-evaluate that information and develop a new plan. Go back to the individual(s) you had review the plan and update them. See what they think.

Always remember that communication is the key. It is not possible to over-communicate.

Continue going through the steps constantly refining your plan and your relationship. Continuous improvement is something that takes time and effort. You cannot expect everything to miraculously change overnight. Don't stop until you are satisfied that your relationship with your boss has improved.

11

The Nuclear Option

"Find peace in what you cannot change."
— ***Unknown***

If you are at this stage and have an
Ogre, then you need to admit your
boss has no interest in working in a
positive manner. Remember, the
only behavior you can change is
your own and the only person that
can make you feel the way you do
is you. You need to either accept
your situation and learn to live with
it or implement the Nuclear Option.

At this point you have limited options. They include:
- Discuss the situation with their boss, the one above
  your boss
- Go to Human Resources
- Consult an attorney or government agency
- Quit

The Boss's Boss

Choosing this option will depend on how open your boss's superior is to meeting employees at your level. It will also depend on what kind of boss that person is. Are they a Bad Boss?

You should expect to hear support for your boss. But a good boss will at least hear you out and try to correct the situation. Bring your documentation. Bring your plan. Carefully explain the behavior you are concerned about and what steps you have taken including meeting with your boss and the results of that meeting.

Finally, tell their boss that you are concerned about retaliation if the Bad Boss finds out about this meeting. That is, if you actually are worried. This is a very real concern, especially if their boss simply says, "I'll talk with them." However, not much can be accomplished if their boss does not intervene.

A boss will often tell their subordinate, your boss, of the meeting and ask that action be taken to correct the situation. This can sometimes have a negative effect. On many occasions, my boss has come to me with concerns raised by my staff and not necessarily addressed at me. (No, I'm not perfect.) But I would use this conversation to directly address the problem at hand.

The danger here is that the boss will get no more than a slap on the wrist and proceed to retaliate in covert ways. In this case, the situation could actually get worse. However, if their superior is a good boss, they will address retaliation immediately and monitor the situation.

Human Resources

Another avenue is to go to the Human Resources department. Human Resources is there to protect both the company and the employee, normally. They should at least listen in confidence and offer advice. Most organizations cannot afford a Bad Boss and will do something about it.

Just as you would when going to your boss's superior, take along your evidence, notes, and anything else you need as a backup when you are discussing the situation.

Let the HR person know you are concerned about retaliation. Get their advice on what to do if this takes place.

Legal

If your boss has broken the law, you need to report it. You should report it to both their boss and Human Resources. Remember that you are protected from retaliation by whistle-blower laws. However, if no action is taken or you feel it would not be productive to go to their boss or Human Resources, you may need to report the actions to a government agency or consult with an attorney.

Consult with a government agency especially if you think there has been illegal discrimination, sexual harassment, wage issues, safety issues, or anything else that may be illegal. You should be able to do an internet search for the appropriate agency that can help you file a complaint.

You can also go to see an attorney. Many lawyers will consult with you for free or at a reduced fee to determine if you have a case. If you do have a case, a lot will depend upon what you want to do and how much money you have to pay the attorney.

Quit

The final option is to quit. Find another job or transfer internally if possible. Put your resume together and move on. You have done all you could. Regardless, get away from the toxic environment and your Bad Boss. If you are going to file for unemployment insurance, make sure to review the rules in your location. In many jurisdictions, if you quit your job you are not entitled to payments. However, leaving though may be the only way to live a healthier and happier life.

12

The Biggest Secret Weapon Is You

"If we all did the thing, we are capable of doing, we would literally astound ourselves."
— Thomas Alva Edison

There is one key to overcoming a Bad Boss that is often misunderstood or ignored. That key is You! Your boss isn't going to change unless they see the need to. You can help them do this. You can also adjust your own thinking and actions to make life with your boss a little better.

Let's face it, our job is to make our boss happy and make them look good. To do so, you often need to do things you don't want to do. Take on tasks you don't want to take on. Say things you do not want to say. We all do this, but take care not to compromise your integrity or your morals. We all have opinions and points of view. Yours are no less valid than your boss's. But remember that, in most cases they have the final word. I have a saying that I'll do anything my boss asks as long as it is not illegal, immoral, or unsafe.

What it comes down to is that only you can change your situation. You can take action as I have suggested in this book or change the way you think about the situation. Only you can change how you feel. Only you can decide to take action.

Be thoughtful. Come up with your plan and follow it through. If necessary, and if everything else fails, find another position. There are plenty of jobs out there with good bosses. Go out and find one!

Good luck on your journey.

Appendix 1
My Plan

Use the following to develop your own plan. Feel free to edit as you need to.

My Plan					Date:		
My boss is…							
	Deer	Control Freak	Bully	Optics Freak	My Buddy	Outlaw	Ogre
Check here							
My goal is to…							
1							
2							
3							
I think my boss wants… (Your boss's goals)							
1							
2							
3							
My boss exhibits the following bad behaviors…							
1							
2							
3							
When my boss exhibits negative behaviors, I feel…							
1							
2							
3							

What am I doing that may be contributing to this situation?

What are some things I can do to make things better?

What strategies am I going to use?

You can download the template at
mikesbooks.com/bad-boss

Appendix 2
Case Studies With Questions

The case studies on the following pages are meant to help you hone your skills at identifying the type of Bad Boss you may be dealing with.

They should also help to get you thinking about what you would do in each situation. Look at what strategies you would implement and use the Seven Steps to develop a long-lasting solution.

Keep in mind that there are no right or wrong answers.

Shari

Shari was an administrative assistant at a large non-profit organization. She was good at her job and got rave reviews at performance appraisal time. She was fast, efficient and accurate.

Her supervisor, Lee, announced his retirement and his job was posted. Shari talked with Lee before he left about the job and decided to go ahead and apply for it. After her interview, Shari was given the position, though she had no experience in supervision. She started immediately.

Shari's first week on the job was great. Everyone was supportive and appreciative of the fact that "one of theirs" was promoted.

Trouble started in the second week, when Shari had several reports to do. Well, these were not tasks she had done before. She was unsure what to do. Fill them out to the best of her ability? She tried to ask her immediate supervisor, but he didn't have time for her.

Her immediate supervisor was very demanding and not pleased with the result of her efforts and told her she needed to figure it out. Shari tried to say that Teresa, one of her subordinates, was to blame for giving her bad information.

Shari had also inherited an employee who was routinely late and left early. That behavior continued after Shari was promoted. She wasn't sure how to deal with the situation, so she did nothing.

67

The team was unhappy with the situation. They had thought Shari would handle it. They were tired of picking up the slack for the tardy employee.

No matter how hard she tried, Shari could not seem to get anything right, and it didn't seem as though her supervisor was willing to help. The once-happy, efficient and accurate employee was now frustrated and stressed and often missed deadlines.

Here are a few questions to think about:
1. What type of Bad Boss is Shari?
2. Are there other types of Bad Bosses here? Which ones, who and why?
3. What should her supervisor be doing?
4. What steps should Shari be taking?
5. Is there anything her staff could do to help?
6. What would you do?

Esperanza

Then there's the case of Esperanza. Esperanza is a business analyst. She was preparing a spreadsheet for her boss. She spent hours getting everything just right. When it came time to present the spreadsheet the boss  reviewed it and gave it back with changes. This happened a total of 17 times. The requested changes included what font to use, line width used in the border and number formatting. It even got to the point where she made changes and then had to change things back to the way they were originally. Finally, she was able to stop, but only because of a deadline. This pattern was repeated on multiple occasions with a variety of projects.

Here are a few questions to think about:
1. What type of Bad Boss does Esperanza have?
2. Are there other types of Bad Bosses here? Which ones and why?
3. What strategies could Esperanza use to help her in this situation?
4. Think about what sort of plan Esperanza should develop.
5. What would you do?

Jack and Nancy

Jack is a financial analyst for a relatively large firm. His boss, Nancy, wants to know everything Jack is doing. She tracks when he comes to work and leaves, even though he is salaried, doesn't have to punch a clock and often works weekends.

She also told him to copy her on any emails he sent out, to keep track of what he was doing. She wants daily meetings to be briefed on what he's doing. Jack feels as though he spends all his time telling her what he is doing and gets nothing accomplished.

She often tells him "I'm leaving this task for you to complete on your own. Go to it." But then she stops by his desk every few hours to see how it is going and to provide her suggestions for her way of doing things. She also asks for daily written updates in addition to the daily meeting.

When Jack is in meetings with Nancy and her boss, she takes credit for his work but blames Jack if anything has gone wrong.

Jack has had it. He can no longer put up with Nancy looking over his shoulder and constantly taking credit for his work, with little positive feedback.

Here are a few questions to think about:
1. What type of Bad Boss is Nancy?
2. Are there other types of Bad Bosses here? Which ones, and why?
3. What strategies could Jack use to help himself?
4. Should Jack develop a plan and go talk with Nancy? Why or why not?
5. What would you do?

Selena

Selena had been at her new job for only six weeks. Her first four weeks were supposed to be training, but she was placed with an individual, Bob, who clearly didn't want to help her. He swore at Selena and started to tell other staff members negative things about her. This was on her third day with the company.

Other staff members told her to talk to the manager about it but failed to tell her that Bob was one of her boss's favorites. She talked to her boss about the situation but quickly regretted it. The manager was no help and dismissed her complaints and told her she just needed to get along.

She was given the cold shoulder afterwards. Her manager would walk past her desk without comment but make a point of going to everyone else on the team and to inquire how they were doing.

Other people got lots of support and encouragement, but not Selena. When the manager and Selena talked, the conversations were typically short and his answers to questions one syllable. The manager would glare at Selena during these conversations, making her very uncomfortable.

After a few more days, Selena was reassigned to a different area but under the same manager, at a lower-level job. Her training was suspended before it finished.

The manager would come over to the new area and chat briefly with everyone there. On one occasion, the manager stood behind Selena's chair, talking with the area supervisor. The manager proceeded to swear repeatedly and loudly.

Selena was told by a co-worker that others there had been treated the same way. Selena is at her wits' end.

Here are a few questions to think about:
1. What type of Bad Boss does Selena have? Be specific.
2. Are there other types of Bad Bosses here? Which ones and why?
3. What strategies can Selena implement?
4. Develop a plan for Selena to go talk with her boss.
5. Could there be anything illegal going on?
6. What would you do?

Duncan

Duncan was a mid-level manager for a large grocery chain. Duncan's boss always seemed on edge, but when he got angry, he lashed out. He was notorious for yelling and always spoke loudly. Duncan was working on the quarterly report one day when the boss came in angrier than usual.

When he stopped by Duncan's desk to review the report, he got angry and yelled about the way Duncan had formatted the report. He threw the papers at Duncan and told him to start over. Oh, and he wanted the report done by lunch.

Here are a few questions to think about:
1. What type of boss does Duncan have?
2. Are there other types of Bad Bosses here? Which ones, and why?
3. What strategies could Duncan start?
4. Should Duncan try to talk with his boss?
5. What would you do?

Anita and Jerry

Anita was excited to get out of the Snow Belt and move to a new job in sunny Southern California.

She was going to work for a large firm in the communications department. She was going to help produce in-house training videos for the company's employees and really looking forward to the work.

During her initial training, she heard fellow employees use terms like "rude," "abrupt," and "sarcastic" to describe Jerry, her new boss. They would tell horror stories about what he was like. She just thought it was typical gossip and ignored what they said.

When she went to work for Jerry, Anita found that all of the gossip was true. Jerry's condescending tone was difficult to deal with. He picked at her for every little thing she did. If she tried to explain anything, he interrupted her. If she got something wrong, he would raise his voice and chew her out. She was not the only victim of Jerry's tantrums.

After about three months, Jerry called Anita into his office and proceeded to yell at her for not finishing a report on time. It was an hour late. He kept her late, even though her shift ended earlier. Worse yet, he said he was not going to pay her.

This was not the first time he had yelled at her. He did it quite often with Anita and many other employees. He invaded her personal space and yelled. Jerry would start out as being condescending but gradually escalated to full-fledged yelling.

Well, Anita had had enough. She leaned close into Jerry but didn't say anything. She just looked at him. Jerry immediately called Human Resources and insisted the director come down immediately. He wanted Anita fired immediately.

The HR director suggested that Anita be moved to another department while they looked for a replacement. Jerry quickly said no. He repeated that she needed to be fired. The HR director said no, and that would not be appropriate.

The HR director asked her if she could stay in Jerry's department to train her replacement before they moved her. She reluctantly said OK.

After she left for lunch and called her husband, her husband suggested that she not go back to work. He had noticed the stress she had been under over the past couple of months and how it had affected her well-being. She had been tired, depressed and stressed out for months now. So, with the support of her spouse, she resigned.

Here are a few questions to think about:
1. What kind of Bad Boss is Jerry?
2. Was Anita justified in leaning in while being yelled at? What does this action mean?
3. Do you think it was appropriate to move Anita? Was there any illegal or inappropriate behavior?
4. What else could Anita have done?
5. Did Human Resources act appropriately?
6. What would you do?

Bruce

Bruce loves himself above all others. He drives the latest Mercedes Benz. He brags about his house and country club membership. He works 12 hours a day and constantly worries about how he looks to upper management. In the process, he makes his staff miserable.

He repeatedly talks about the optics of what they do and how it's important to present a good image. Bruce is always spouting words of wisdom to his staff and pretends to listen when his staff offer suggestions, but he never follows through with any of them.

He talks about how smart he is and how he attended an ivy league school. He doesn't mention that he barely graduated.

He also likes to criticize others. It could be for their work, their appearance, or even their personal quirks.

Here are a few questions to think about:
1. What type of Bad Boss is Bruce?
2. What should his staff do?
3. What would you do?

Jenny

Jenny was a surgical technician at a local regional hospital. A single mom of three, she lived in a small town about 25 miles from the hospital.

She had been having trouble with her supervisor for some time.

On one occasion, there was a tremendous down pour that flooded all of the roads to the hospital. Jenny called in and said she could not get to work because of the flooding and the roads were not clear.

When she arrived at work the next day, she was called into the Human Resources office at the end of her shift. The HR director, a 27-year-old with little experience, and the supervisor proceeded to give her an oral warning for arriving late. They kept her over her shift and did not pay her for the extra time.

She was later called in again and told she had a "bad attitude." She got along great with all of the doctors, other techs and nurses. The supervisor could provide no examples of misbehavior or "attitude."

Jenny had finally had it and found another job in another state. During her exit interview, she was asked to stay late on her last day of work and indicated they would not pay her.

Here are a few questions to think about:
1. What kind of Bad Boss did Jenny have?
2. Do you think it was appropriate to call Jenny into HR?
3. Was there any illegal or inappropriate behavior going on?
4. Did Human Resources act appropriately?
5. What would you do?

Jim Johnson

Jim Johnson was a 37-year-old supervisor in a huge retail operation. He had been promoted over numerous other managers after just four and a half years with the business. A number of his peers believed Jim's promotion to department head had more to do with workplace politics and also "sucking up" to the company president than it did from specific professional achievements. Although some people were resentful, many were also impressed with Jim's personality, looks and success.

Jim's spouse was attractive as well as the mother of their two youngsters. Her parents were successful local business owners and also enjoyed spending their money on their daughter and her family. There were that his wife's family paid for Jim's expensive cars, snazzy house and elite golf club subscription.

Jim's subordinates were increasingly upset with him. His department did not seem cohesive and no one worked together as a team. Members of his group assumed that Jim really did not care for them or their professional development.

They thought their work assignments were primarily aimed at progressing Jim's career and making him look good. They also thought that Jim was sacrificing quality and efficiency for his own short-term advantage.

Jim sometimes used his group meetings as a personal platform to pontificate about his grand ideas and for blatant discussions of his individual power, brilliance and plans for future success. Despite his success, he was hypersensitive to criticism. There was unanimous agreement that he was intolerant of even the most useful advice.

Regardless, Jim still had his fans. He definitely sought out those in power and was able to play politics. Although he appeared to tolerate subordinates that might be valuable to him, he seemed to have little concern for others under him. Those who worked for him often felt valued for a while, but at some point, wound up feeling used and abused.

Here are a few questions to think about:
1. What type of Bad Boss is Jim?
2. Are there other types of Bad Bosses here? Which ones and why?
3. Was Jim simply ambitious?
4. What should upper management be doing?
5. What should his staff do to work for Jim?
6. What would you do?

Hope

Hope was the supervisor for a small accounting team at the local hospital. Hope liked her team and thought the world of them. She really enjoyed spending time out of her office talking with the staff. They would often discuss last night's TV episode of their favorite show.

She knew the names of all of their children and significant others. She went to lunch with members of her staff and even bought birthday gifts for some of them. Hope often invited the team over to her house for dinner or cookouts. Fridays were reserved for drinks after work and everyone was expected to attend. If someone missed the Friday night gathering, Hope made sure her disappointment was noticed.

Because she spent so much time out of her office, Hope's work suffered. She would assign much of it to the staff members she didn't care for as much. The staff lacked time to take on these assignments because Hope would spend so much time talking to them.

Some of her staff became increasingly concerned with the preferential treatment some others appeared to be getting. Those got the easy work assignments along with birthday gifts and free lunches.

Morale was quickly declining.

Here are a few questions to think about:
1. · What type of Bad Boss is Hope?
2. Are there other types of Bad Bosses here? Which ones, and why?
3. What could her staff do?
4. Think about developing a plan for Hope's staff.
5. Should they meet with her as a group?
6. What would you do?

Appendix 3
Common Traits of Bad Bosses and Some Fast Fixes

You can download the template here or at mikesbooks.com/bad-boss

Bad Boss	Traits	What Can You Do?
Deer in the Headlights	Indecision Lack of commitment Makes mistakes Does not understand policies or procedures Overly friendly	Support them/be encouraging Subtly suggest what they can do to improve Avoid talking negatively about them in front of others
Control Freak	Setting too many priorities Need for frequent progress updates Blaming others Need to know the details and be involved in them	Be professional Let them know you can do the work Be appreciative of their attempts to provide direction Make sure they understand your

Bad Boss	Traits	What Can You Do?
	Measuring too many things	skills and your competencies
	Difficulty delegating	Be proactive
	Building too much consensus	Have a discussion about how and when your Bad Boss wants updates or briefings
	Secrecy	
	Intervening too much	
		Communicate
The Bully	They need to be heard	Communicate
	May yell at any little thing	Observe their behavior
	No regard for your feelings	Repeat back their instructions to show you understand
	Don't care about their employees	
	Passive-aggressive	Listen carefully and pay attention
	Subtle and not so subtle put-downs	Do your best
	Avoids confrontation	Tell them that the raised voices make you uncomfortable
	Makes you doubt or question yourself	Stay calm

Bad Boss	Traits	What Can You Do?
	Procrastinates	Set boundaries
	Manipulative	Document
		Be strong
		Re-assess why you love your job
		Seek positive reinforcement from co-workers and friends
		Talk to your boss
Optics Freak	A sense of entitlement	Stay on their good side
	Unusually charismatic	Compliment them
	Can attack ruthlessly if criticized	Be professional
	Requires excessive admiration and loyalty	Communicate
	Believes they are special	
	Uses other people	
	Displays superior attitudes and behaviors	

Bad Boss	Traits	What Can You Do?
	Has grandiose sense of self-importance Yearns for unlimited success and power Lacks empathy Is compensating for low self-esteem	
My Buddy	Wants to be friends Plays favorites Wants to socialize Wants to know personal details of your life Spends more time socializing then working	Be professional Set boundaries Be polite and respectful
The Outlaw	Ignores rules Does not consider consequences	Go to Human Resources Get legal advice

Bibliography

Benjamin, Kimberly A., (June 24, 2013). "6 Steps to Conflict Resolution in the Workplace". Retrieved from HR Daily Advisor: https://hrdailyadvisor.blr.com/2013/06/24/6-steps-to-conflict-resolution-in-the-workplace/

Chappelow, Craig, Peter Royane, Bill Adams. *The Toxic Boss Survival Guide - Tactics for Navigating the Wilderness at Work*. Center for Creative Leadership. Kindle Edition.

Flaxington, Beverly D., (February 12, 2018). "Dealing with a Difficult Boss." Retrieved from Psychology Today: https://www.psychologytoday.com/us/blog/understand-other-people/201802/dealing-difficult-boss

Gaille, B. (2017, May 28). "9 Shocking Statistics About Bad Bosses." Retrieved from Brandon Gaille Small Business & Marketing Advice: https://brandongaille.com/8-shocking-statistics-about-bad-bosses/

Hayden, Jeff, (May 12, 2014). "Top 50 Management and Leadership Experts." Inc. Magazine website: https://www.inc.com/jeff-haden/the-top-50-leadership-and-management-experts-mon.html?cid=search

Lipman, Victor, (August 4, 2015). "People Leave Managers, Not Companies." Retrieved from Forbes: https://www.forbes.com/sites/victorlipman/2015/08/04/people-leave-managers-not-companies/

Mendoza, Charley. (April 25, 2018). "How to Deal with a Difficult Boss (7 Top Strategies)." Retrieved from EnvatoTuts+:

https://business.tutsplus.com/tutorials/how-to-deal-with-a-difficult-boss-7-top-strategies--cms-31009

Niaz, Asma. (December 19, 2017). "10 Brilliant Tips for Dealing with a Difficult Boss." From Insights for Professionals: https://www.insightsforprofessionals.com/den-us/management/leadership/tips-for-dealing-with-a-difficult-boss

Phillpott, Siôn. (November 22, 2017). "11 Types of Bad Bosses and How to Deal with Them." Retrieved from Career Addict: https://www.careeraddict.com/deal-bad-boss

Potter, Robert. (2014). *Coping with Your Boss from Hell.* Robert L. Potter, LLC.

Rao, Kathleen. (2014). *My Boss is a Jerk.* LC Publishing LLC.

Ripper, Becky. (January 24, 2019). "The Big, Bad Boss: Poor Management Costly." Retrieved from The Business Times: http://thebusinesstimes.com/the-big-bad-boss-poor-management-costly/

Stephens, Stephanie. (July 15, 2012). "Work it Out: Dealing with a Difficult Boss." Retrieved from WebMD: https://www.webmd.com/mental-health/features/dealing-with-a-difficult-boss#1

Winfrey, G. (2015, August 29). "Why Most Managers are Wrong for Their Roles." Retrieved from Inc.: https://www.inc.com/graham-winfrey/why-most-bosses-shouldn-t-be-bosses-in-the-first-place.html

Handy References

The following are handy references if you want more help in the leadership and growth world. (I am receiving no compensation for any of these.)

John Maxwell is a giant in leadership and growth. You can get his books at his store or on Amazon.com. Here is the address to his store:

store.johnmaxwell.com/

Dr. Maxwell also has his own team of trainers, speakers and coaches that can deliver inspiring presentations and course. (Full disclosure: I am one of them.) You can find the John Maxwell Team at the following link:

johnmaxwellgroup.com/

Still another John Maxwell link is at:

corporatesolutions.johnmaxwell.com/

Stephen R. Covey is also a giant in the field. You can find his books on Amazon or at:

franklincovey.com/books.html

There are many other great writers in the leadership field. These are just two that I particularly enjoy.

Here's a list of Inc. magazine's top fifty leadership writers from the Inc. website. Take a look. There are ton of great books as well as videos by these leadership experts.

1. John C. Maxwell
2. Seth Godin
3. Jack Welch
4. Guy Kawasaki
5. Tim Ferriss
6. Daniel Goleman
7. Dale Carnegie
8. Kenneth H. Blanchard
9. Chris Hallberg
10. Michael E. Porter
11. Marshall Goldsmith
12. Tom Peters
13. Stephen R. Covey
14. Robin Sharma
15. Simon Sinek
16. Patrick Lencioni
17. Rosabeth Moss Kanter
18. Tony Hsieh
19. Thomas L. Friedman
20. Orrin Woodward
21. Steve Farber
22. Don Tapscott
23. Clayton M. Christensen
24. David Allen
25. Brian Tracy
26. Bob Sutton
27. Michael Hyatt
28. John P. Kotter
29. Peter F. Drucker
30. Eric Ries
31. Anthony Robbins

32. Gary Hamel
33. Mike Myatt
34. Jason Fried
35. Charles Duhigg
36. Daniel H. Pink
37. Dan Rockwell
38. Marcus Buckingham
39. Chris Brady
40. Jurgen Appelo
41. Robert B. Cialdini
42. John Baldoni
43. Jeffrey Gitomer
44. Gretchen Rubin
45. Malcolm Gladwell
46. Susan Cain
47. Dan Ariely
48. Jim Collins
49. Liz Strauss
50. Chris Brogan

One Final Thing...

I would really appreciate it if you would review my book on Amazon.

Also, you can drop me a line or ask me questions by emailing me at:

mamiller1101@outlook.com

Don't forget that, as your "thank-you" for getting this book, I'd like to give you a free gift: a unique PDF called Leadership Strategies available at:

mikesbooks.space/bad-boss/

Also, don't forget the downloads for the appendices at the following page:

mikesbooks.space/bad-boss/

Index

Notes

Notes

Notes

Notes